In the Name of Allah, the Gracious, the Merciful

Copyright © 2022 Somayeh Zomorodi

All rights reserved.
No part of this publication may be reproduced, distributed, or transmitted in any form or by any means, including photocopying, recording, or other electronic or mechanical methods, without the prior written permission of the publisher, except in the case of brief quotations embodied in critical reviews and certain other noncommercial uses permitted by copyright law. For permission requests, write to the publisher, addressed "Attention: - Permissions (Be like the Stars and rise)," at the email address below.

 A catalogue record for this book is available from the National Library of Australia

Lantern Publications
info@lanternpublications.com
www.lanternkids.com.au
"Lantern Kids" is a subsidiary of Lantern Publications

Ordering Information:

Quantity sales. Special discounts are available on quantity purchases by corporations, associations, and others. For details, contact the distributor at the address below.

ISBN: 978-1-922583-40-6

First Edition

Illustrations: Zahra Nabaei | **Editor:** Dr Abidali Mohamedali and Sis Sabrina Mohamedali

I'm thankful to Elina Batool who helped in translation of these precious words

To my children
Mohammad Mahdi
Fatemeh Zahra
Fatemeh Narjes
&
All children anywhere in the world

My dear,

Now that you have gone through the years of childhood and are becoming a young adult, I wanted to give you a precious gift that, when it is discovered, you find in it all the beauty and goodness in the world.

That precious gift is friendship with God.

Who is better and more worthy of Allah for this friendship!

And what other way is better than praying and talking with God to enjoy his friendship!!

Allah the Almighty revealed to David: "*O David! Send my message to the people of the earth, I am the friend of someone who is my friend, and I am the associate of someone who is my associate and companion with the one who mentions me, and I am accompanied by my servant who is with me ... And whenever a servant loves me, I understand his love from his heart for me. I love him in a manner that no other of my servants has ever loved him...*"[1]

My dear,

The world and everything in it; the joy and sorrow, the victories and the failures- are perishable and will one day disappear.

Soon, everything will end, just like the summer vacation at the end of which you said, "It passed so quickly..."

The world is also passing fast, but what remains for you, all your hardships and even your happiness, is your peace of mind and your friendship with God.

He can be your Savior, He can be your intimate friend, and help you in a more Merciful way than your parents ...

Never neglect to pray Salaat because prayer is the place of meeting with your kind friend, Allah the Almighty.

And remember, **"all of us will return to God."**[2]

My sweetheart,

Look at the sky at night, when the moon shines in the middle of the black curtain which surrounds it. It is just like the moment in which you are on the prayer mat, praying in front of the Merciful God. You are bright and glowing just like the moon, when you pray!

Someone asked Imam Sādiq ﷺ: *"Why is Sayyida Fāṭima called Zahrā?"* The Imam ﷺ replied: *"For Fāṭima, peace be upon her, was one who, when she stood in her mihrāb (for worshipping and saying her prayers), her light shone for the inhabitants of the Heavens as stars shine for the inhabitants of the earth."* [3]

My lovely child,

Be aware! Prayer will bring you close to a God who is the best friend, Most Merciful companion, and the best listener.

He says in the Holy Quran: "**We are closer to him than his neck-vein.**"[4]

He is the God who is always present and will never leave you alone.

At any moment and every hour, He sees you and hears you...

So speak to Him ...

Talk to the one who is the kindest.

Who is better and more meritorious than Allah the Gracious for friendship?!!

Someone came to the Prophet and asked: *"Is Allah near to us that we need to pray with Him, or is He far?"*

Then Allah. the Wise, revealed this verse to his dear messenger "**When My servants ask you about Me, [tell them that] I am indeed near. I answer the supplicant's call when he calls Me....**"[5]

My sweetheart,

Look carefully at God's creations. He created the mountains to be mighty, steadfast holders of the land, the productive green trees, and the rivers flowing and life-giving to all the creatures. More complete than this, is the creation of the Earth and the Galaxy, the seasons, the days, and the night...

However, God called man the best, best of all, to the point where he commanded the angels to prostrate on the greatness of his creation.

So, thank God...

It is time to thank Him for all the blessings He has created for you. Blessings that you can never count.

Allah, the Almighty, says:

> **"Have they not seen that We have created cattle for them—of what Our hands have worked—so they have become their masters? And We made them tractable for them; some of them make their mounts, and some of them eat. There are other benefits for them therein, and drinks. Will they not then give thanks?"**[6]

And what worship and practice are better, more complete, and more loveable for being grateful to the Almighty God except for Salaat?

My dear,

Prayer is beloved. It's a favourite of Allah the Almighty. Do you know that when all the good things are gathered in something, it becomes loved! A good prayer becomes the light of the eye of the Prophet ﷺ. It becomes like delicious food for the hungry and fresh water for the thirsty.

The Prophet ﷺ said to Abu Dhar[7]:

> "O, Abu Dhar! God Almighty has made prayer the light of my eyes and made it so dear to me that the hungry love delicious food, and the thirsty love fresh water. When the hungry man eats, he will eventually be satisfied, but I would never get satiated from prayer."[8]

The Prophet loves something that God loves, and Allah, the Merciful, loves prayer more than any other practice of His servants.

Imam Sādiq ؏ says:

> "The most loved act near Almighty God is prayer...Surely, when he prostrates himself and prostrates for a long time, Iblees[9] raises his voice, 'Woe to me! He obeyed God, and I rebelled, he prostrated himself to God, and I refused.'"[10]

Imam Ali ؏ also says:

> "No action pleases Allah the Almighty more than prayer. So let the world`s business not distract you from your prayer time...."[11]

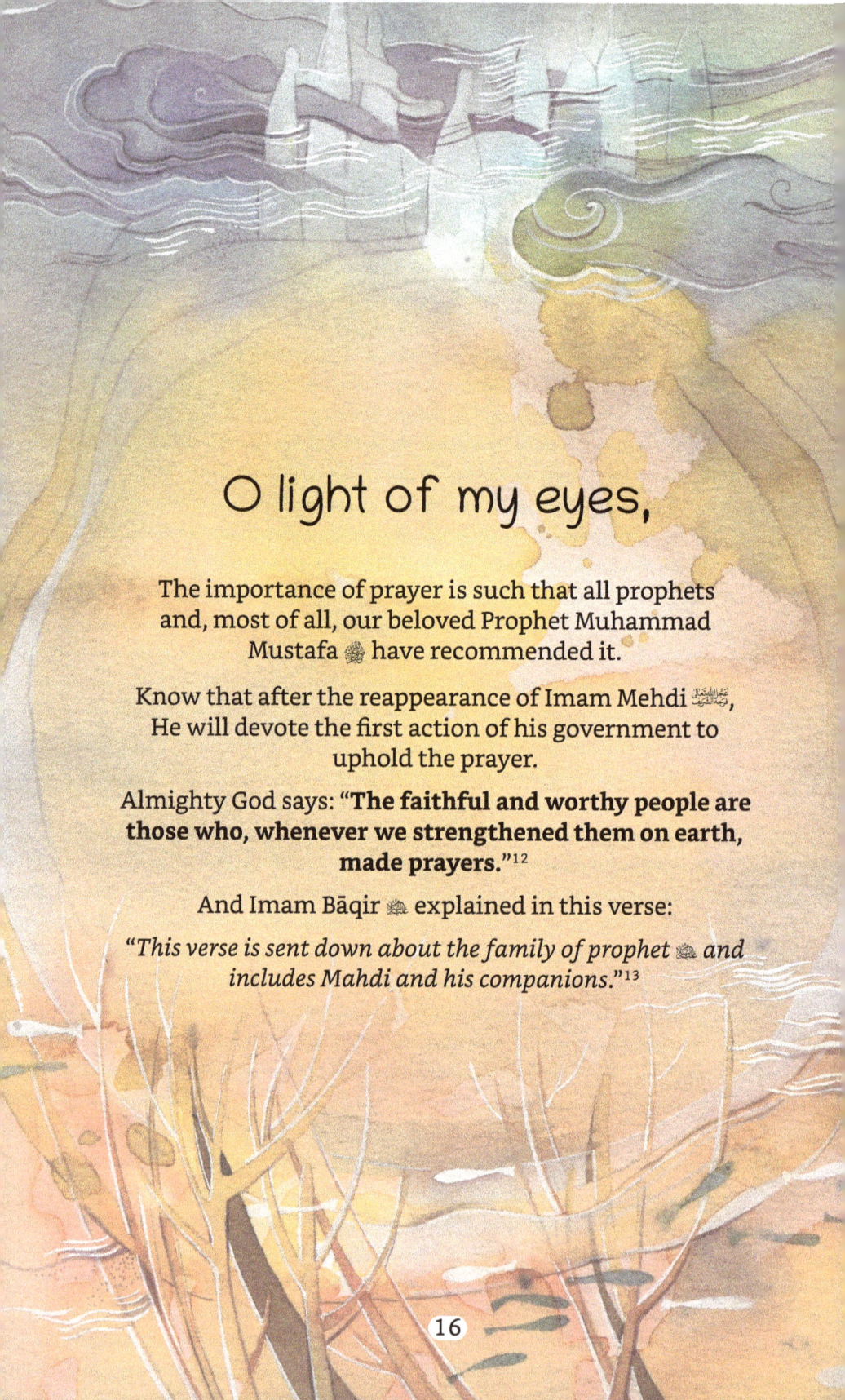

O light of my eyes,

The importance of prayer is such that all prophets and, most of all, our beloved Prophet Muhammad Mustafa ﷺ have recommended it.

Know that after the reappearance of Imam Mehdi ﷺ, He will devote the first action of his government to uphold the prayer.

Almighty God says: **"The faithful and worthy people are those who, whenever we strengthened them on earth, made prayers."**[12]

And Imam Bāqir ﷺ explained in this verse:

"This verse is sent down about the family of prophet ﷺ and includes Mahdi and his companions."[13]

Imam Mahdi ﷺ is a restorer of religion and prayer, and one of the goals of the Imam`s government is to establish prayer.

Even Imam Husain ؑ performed his Salaat with his companions on the day of Ashura on the battlefield.

And Imam Ali ؑ, the true Imam, repeatedly looked at the sky in the battle of Siffin to see when the time for the noon prayer would be.

My child,

Prayer will light up your face.

On the day of Resurrection, the face of the one who prayed (muswalli) will be enlightened with the light of prayer. The first question on the day of Resurrection will be from prayer, and one who did not perform prayer will be punished.

Let me tell you a story from the Qur'an:

The people of heaven were in pleasant gardens. Whatever they wished and determined was prepared for them: a variety of foods, fruits, beverages and…slaves served them. There was no fatigue, boredom, sadness, or grief at all.

They were supposed to be eternally in this lovely and blessed place, and how happy they were …!

The people in heaven then, for a moment, looked down. The horrible condition of hell was intolerable. They looked at each other and said, 'all this punishment is for what sin?' they asked each other. With surprise, one of the dwellers of Paradise pointed to one of the inhabitants of hell and said: 'I know him, we were together in a school and a place, but I don't know why he is there.' He involuntarily turned towards him and asked, 'Why are you in hell? Why do you suffer so much? What sin did you do?'

He and some of his companions came out of the fire and, with great pain and trouble, said: "**We were not among those who prayed…**"[14]

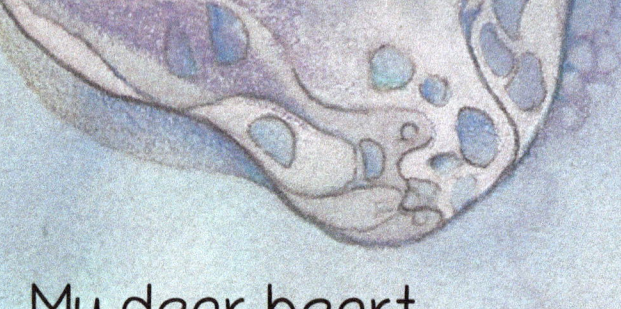

My dear heart,

In life, there are two ways one can choose to go;

The way of God, which is the truth, brings you prosperity and happiness in the world and the hereafter...

The other is the path of Satan, which is false and invites you to fire, misery, and darkness.

Consider which way you want to choose before deciding to do any work.

So, in companionship and friendship with people, in which direction do you wish to go? Where do you walk with them?

Are they the ones who perform prayers and are friends with God?! Or not ... do their actions pull away from the goodness, purity, satisfaction and grace of the Merciful God?

Those who were friends with a person and a group who pulled them away from the remembrance of God will say on the Day of Resurrection when they see the result of their actions:

"I wish there had been between me and you, the distance between the east and the west, what an evil companion."[15]

In prayer, we also ask God to guide us to the right path, His own path.

And what a prettier and greener way, more pleasant than the road on the side of God!!!

And what is a better and easier vehicle than prayer to reach God!!!

My dearest,

If we knew that in prayer we are speaking with such a great creator, Gracious, Mighty, Wise, Compassionate and Generous, we would never be mentally absent, and we would not think about anything else.

Say:

> "Indeed, I have turned my face toward Him who created the heavens and the earth as a Hanīf, and I am not one of the polytheists."[16]

Imam Bāqir ﷺ said: *"When you are in prayer, pay full attention to your prayer. The more you have the presence of your heart and attention, the more your prayer will be accepted…"*

If you taste the sweetness of prayer, you will not enjoy any other pleasure in the world as good. You cannot replace anything with Salaat.

The pleasure of loving God is the sweetest pleasure that can be experienced in the world, and then you want nothing but the love of God.

The late Ayatollah Bahjat says: "If the world's kings had known the pleasure of worship, they would never have sought material means. "

My dear,

Prayer has many effects and blessings. Both Qur'anic verses and traditions talk about the impact and benefits of prayer.

We read in the Holy Qur'an:

> **"Indeed the prayer prevents from the immorality and evil deeds…."**[17]

Imam Sādiq ﷺ says:

> *"Anyone who likes to know whether his prayer is accepted, see whether his prayer has prevented him from doing sin. His prayer is accepted as much as his prayer has prevented him from doing sin."*[18]

When you feel pleasure in conversing and praying with God, you are not interested in committing sin anymore and offending your kind friend.

You want to be as He likes and has commanded, which is obligatory for your happiness and prosperity.

Prayer strengthens you against Satan's temptation and the gravity of sin; do not be deceived.

A prayer you offer with attention and pleasure and knowing whom you are standing before, will be your Savior.

My Child!

Prayer is the opportunity for repentance and remission of sins...

Our Prophet said:

> "If one of you has a river in your home which contains pure water, and he washes himself five times a day, is there anything on the body of impurity and dirt?

They replied: No

Then the Prophet then said:

> "Prayer is just like this flowing water. Every time someone offers a prayer, the sins committed between two prayers are wiped away. Similarly, the wounds from sins that settle on his soul are healed due to Salaat, and the rust on his heart is scraped off."[19]

Is there anyone kinder than God?!

We are guilty of sin, wrong and neglect on our part, but God Himself is the forgiving and the Savior.

Salaat-that clear and clean stream-cleans us and gives us life. Everyday prayer rejuvenates the freshness of life in our souls and hearts.

Without water, a human cannot continue his life; without prayer, his soul will die, like a fish that comes out of the water and slowly dies.

My love!

God's mercy is infinite. We can never count God's blessings. If the water of the seas was ink, it would not be enough to write all of His goodness, kindness and infinite blessings.

Look at the kind lap of the mother; a small portion of God's great mercy has been given to the mother.

The relationship between prayer and God's mercy is also very interesting and worth listening to.

Imam Bāqir narrates from the Prophet of God:

> "When a believing servant stands in prayer, God looks at him and turns to him, spreading the shadow of mercy from above his head to the shores of the sky, and taking the angels around him to the shores of the sky, and an angel is placed on top of him that says to him: "O worshiper! If you knew who looks at you and to whom you pray, and will not return, and you will never go out of here."[20]

And Imam Ali said: "When a person stands in prayer, the devil comes and looks at him enviously because he sees God's mercy has surrounded him."[21]

After your prayer, sit on your prayer mat, let the special mercy of God pour on you like raindrops, and you will be soaked in mercy, pure and forgiven.

As angels have surrounded you up to the heavens, testify to the unity of God and thank him and deny every bad word that critics and disbelievers have said (since God is blameless of such words).

And these Adhkar are repeated in the Tasbih of Sayyida Fāṭima Zahra; Allah is the greatest (*Allahu Akbar*) 34 times, Thank God (*alhamdullilah*) 33 times and Glory be to Allah (*Subhanallah*) 33 times.[22]

My dearest,

The world and what is in it keep us very busy and entertained.

Sometimes we are so busy that we forget God, The God who has created us, and all that is good, and all the blessings He bestowed on us. With His Mercy, He kept us from evil and guided us towards prosperity.

What an evil end will we have if we are neglectful and forgetful of God.

Imam al-Ridha ﷺ said:

> "Salaat was obligatory every day and night, so that man did not forget his master and creator, and so that eventually forgetfulness does not cause him to wander and then revolt and oppress. And prayer was obligatory so that human beings would be obedient to God. As he stands in front of God, it causes the prevention of sins and shields and obstructs all kinds of corruption."[23]

Indeed, in the Holy Quran, Allah the Almighty says, **"men whom neither trade nor bargaining distracts from the remembrance of Allah... ."**[24]

Imam Bāqir ﷺ about this verse said:

> "These were the merchants who, because of the time of prayers, left the business and went to prayer, would have more rewards than those who do not trade."[25]

Take care of prayer. Your salvation from neglect and forgetfulness is in prayer. Prayer is an excellent reminder of God.

My Dearest!

It's not easy to become a butterfly.

The silkworm wraps its thin, delicate threads around itself and keeps itself away from ugliness to be beautiful.

You must stay away from the indecency of the world to become beautiful and divine…and this means piety…

The pious one is the butterfly of the garden of beings.

The truthful Imam, Imam Ali, in a great sermon in Nahjul Balagha, mentions lovely words in praise of the pious ones,

"The pious persons bow down and break down in front of their God, spread their wings, and put their foreheads in God's respectful court. They put their palms, knees, and feet on the ground like a praying mat, as if making the ground and themselves one by their humbleness. They complain to God about the world's traps, Satan's temptation, and hell's punishment, and they ask for salvation from God from all of this."[26]

It is not surprising that in the Qur'an, the pious ones are introduced as those who pray.[27]

The relationship between prayer and piety is powerful, like butterflies and flowers that perfectly complement each other. It is salaat that gives you the sweet taste of faith, and then you will find the strength of resistance against evil deeds and sins.

My Child!

Every door needs a key to open, and prayer is the key to heaven's door..

Isn't the real Paradise being alone with your kind creator for some moments…?

And talking to Him in the most perfect form possible- Salaat?

Nothing can take the place of prayer. The light that prayer creates in the soul cannot be created by any other worship, not even an intimate conversation with God.

As the Prophet ﷺ said: *"Prayer is the light of believers."*[28]

And also, Imam Ali ibn Musa al-Ridha ﷺ said: *"Verily, Prayer is the best worshipping to Allah."*[29]

My dearest,

Luqman said in a recommendation to his son:

"O, my son! As soon as you hear the call of prayers, Don't delay it even for any good deed, do your prayers first!...and pray in the congregation even if it's a difficult time for you."

Our beloved Prophet also said: *"The one who delays the prayer will not receive my intercession."*[30]

The time when Imam Sādiq was on his deathbed in the last moments of his life, he requested all his family members to gather so that he could remind them of an important affair. He opened his eyes and said: *"The one who is lazy about prayer and takes it lightly, our intercession will not reach him."*[31]

Do you know how significant this loss is for a man if we miss the opportunity of the intercession of the Prophet and his household?

It is like a garden that does not get irrigated and leafy trees and greens that have dried due to lack of water, we too will perish due to the thirst of intercession.

The life of a believer depends on intercession. Is it possible to live without Prophet and his household!?

Who is more sympathetic to us than Prophet and his household, who recommended prayer on time for our happiness and prosperity.

My love,

In the boundless blue sky, the flight of birds astonishes us; with wings stretched out and flying high above, it seems the infinite sky is their own domain of flight. They just fly out there from one direction to another.

God, the All-Wise, brings this greatness to our attention in the Holy Quran and explains....

> "Do you not see that Allah is exalted by whoever is within the heavens and the earth and [by] the birds with wings spread [in flight]? Each [of them] has known his [means of] prayer and exalting [Him], and Allah knows of what they do."[32]

Sometimes I think that birds have taken a place in the sky so as to glorify Allah, the Almighty. From the height of the sky, the earth and everything in it becomes small, birds, when praising God, fly high in the sky, and the world, under their wings seems small and becomes worthless.

In this way, while praising God (in their prayers), a human being flies high and leaves the world behind, including all its materialistic things.

The Holy Qur'an, in Surah Sād, explains regarding Prophet David...

> "Be patient over what they say and remember Our servant, David, the possessor of strength; indeed, he was one who repeatedly turned back [to Allah]. Indeed, we subjected the mountains [to praise] with him, exalting [Allah] in the [late] afternoon and [after] sunrise. And the birds were assembled, all with him repeating [praises]."[33]

A human who is worshipping God (in prayers) is in harmony with the creatures of the universe, and the creatures of the universe will be at the service of the pure and true worshiper.

My sweetheart,

God created man and made him so great that he placed him as a successor on his land and commanded the angels to prostrate their heads to this greatness…

The angels said: "Lord, do you put someone in the land who will cause corruption and bloodshed while we mention you and embrace your praise?"

The Lord said: "**I know something that you do not know….**"[34]

And He repeatedly mentioned in the Qur'an the high status and goodness of the creation of the human;

> "**Indeed, we have created man in the best of moderation.**"[35]

> "**And truly, we cherished the sons of Adam.**"[36]

> "**Then Praise be to God, the best of the creators.**"[37]

How can a man whose creation is so unique and valuable be contaminated by corruption, destruction and bloodshed? How can he crush his humanity under his feet and hurt others with his hands and tongue? How can he be a slave to his shoes and clothing?

Surely when man moves away from the teachings of the Lord and his messengers will lose his way.

The Holy Prophet ﷺ said: "*My ahlul bayt (people of my house) are amongst my people like the stars in the sky. Every time a star sets, another rises.*"[38]

Keep your eyes on the sky. When you take the footprints of the stars and move, you will not lose your way even in the dark deserts, and when you reach the spring of prayer (Salaat), you will attain eternal life from its tasty water.

My dearest!

Many times before this, I have told you that even if I am not beside you, you are not alone.

"To Allah belongs the East and the West: Wherever you turn, there is the presence of Allah."[39]

Not a drop of rain falls from the sky, but God does not know who quenches his thirst or what grows from it.

No grain in the stalks of wheat reap, and God does not know who it will be served with it.

There is no ray of sunlight that shines without God's permission or command to heat the frozen land.

There is no pain, the medicine and treatment God doesn`t know.

There is no heart which God does not know what is hidden in it, whether it wishes for the joy and happiness of His servants or evil and loss for them.

My mother always said, "A man`s fortune is always based on his intentions."

Yes, my dear, all the issues of the world and the creations are based on this.

An act is based upon intentions.

Worshipping God also demands pure intentions. Even your prayer, if done for the happiness, satisfaction, obedience and love of God, you win, but if it is done for the satisfaction of people and a habit, then a looser is such a worshipper who doesn't achieve the world nor the hereafter.

My Moon!

There will be a time when I will not be beside you, I wrote this for you so that you know and always remember...

From the day I found out that you are being shaped within me up to this day when you have grown tall in front of me like a beautiful sapling and have become mature, I have wanted from God that he makes you taste the sweetness of His love, and wished that He put the Salaat (prayer) by your side and make the Ahlul bayt ﷺ and the Quran which are two expensive trusteeships of the Holy Prophet ﷺ the light of your eyes.

And wish the best for you.

The prayer of a mother will be answered.

The End

References and Notes

1. Kulliyat hadith Qudsi by Sheikh Hur A'meli, V. 1, p. 191; narrates this hadith from the book of Shahid Thani Musakkin al-fuad (published by Lantern Publications)
2. Surah al-Baqara, 2:156
3. Ma'ani al-akhbar, p. 64; Ilal al-sharayi', v. 1, p. 181; Awalim Ul-Uloom, v. 11, p. 63; Nisaa an-Nabi wa Awladeh, p. 92.
4. Surah Qaf 50: 16
5. Surah Baqarah, 2: 186
6. Surah Ya-sin, 36:71-73
7. Abu Dhar was a truthful, strong and pious companion of the Holy Prophet, who from the onset of his conversion to Islam till the last moment of his life, didn't stray from the Path of Truth. He fought against oppression and fully supported Prophethood and wilayah and was among the first people to convert to Islam.
8. Bihar al-Anwar, v. 77, p. 77, Mustadrak al-Wasail, v. 1, p. 174
9. Iblīs (alternatively Eblis or Ibris) is a figure frequently occurring in the Quran, commonly in relation to the creation of Adam and the command to prostrate himself before him. After he refused, he was cast out. Also referred to as Shaytan or Satan.
10. Bihar al-Anwar, v. 78. P. 99
11. Al-Khisal, p. 621
12. Surah Al-Haj, 22:41
13. Bihar al-Anwar, v. 51, p. 47

14 According to Surah Muddathir, Verse 40-43
15 Surah Az-Zukhruf, 43: 38
16 Surah Al-An'am, 6: 79
17 Surah Ankabut, 29:45
18 Bihar al-Anwar, v. 79, p. 198
19 Wasail al-shia, v. 3, p. 7
20 Al-Kafi, v. 3,p. 265, Falah al-Saeel, p. 288
21 Al-Khisal, p. 632, Tuhfatul Uqool, p. 122
22 33 سُبحَانَ الله ,33 الحَمدُلله ,34 الله اکبَر
23 Uyoon Akhbar al-Ridha ؑ., v. 2, p. 104, Ilal al-Sharayie, v. 2, p. 11
24 Surah Nur, Verse 37
25 Mustadrak al-Wasail, v. 3, p. 164
26 Nahjul Balagha, sermon 193, Translated by Muhammed Dashti
27 Surah Baqarah, 2:3
28 Nahjul Fasaha, p. 396
29 Jami`e Ahadith Shia, v. 4, p. 50
30 Amali al-Saduq, p. 399
31 Bihar al-Anwar, v. 47, p. 2
32 Surah an-Nur, 24: 41
33 Surah Sad, 38: 17-19
34 Surah Baqarah, 2: 30
35 Surah Tin, 95: 4
36 Surah Al-Isra, 17: 70
37 Surah Al- Mu'minun, 23: 14
38 Bihar al-Anwar, v. 23, p. 44
39 Surah Baqarah, 2: 115